"Words give us power
to learn and to grow ..."

Best Wishes,

John Bile

"Each of us has a vital role to play, a contribution to make..."
(Excerpts from presentations by author John Gile)

"Children with parents actively involved in their children's education scored 28 points above average in reading while children with low parental involvement scored 46 points below average in national testing cited by the U.S. Secretary of Education. That 74 point spread is about one third of the average score. Those results remind us that helping children develop reading power and all the powers which flow out of reading is a team effort. Parents have about a third of the responsibility, teachers have about a third of the responsibility, and the children themselves have about a third of the responsibility. Each of us has a vital role to play, a contribution to make."

From The Author's Presentation, World Congress, International Reading Association

"Reading changes lives. Reading turned an unschooled river rat into a Mark Twain, a backwoods rail-splitter into a Lincoln, a disruptive troublemaker into a Thomas Edison, a maltreated slave into a Frederick Douglass. Reading changes lives."

Connecticut Interview

"We must do more than teach our children to read; we must *inspire* them to read. We must do more than teach them how to read; we must teach them to *love* to read."

From "Reading: A Bridge Over Troubled Waters"

"Children need play time, dream time, free time, time to explore and think and create. Children with well developed language skills, who have been helped to discover the fun and power of reading and writing, have powerful ways to play, to dream, to be free, to create, to cope."

From "The Language Crisis"

"Fostering self-esteem is important, but challenging children to develop their reading and writing powers is how we foster the real thing. Counterfeit self-esteem is worthless to children who grow up unable to compete in the real world, unable to get and hold a job, unable to do what they want to do and be what they want to be because of inadequate communication skills. We help develop real, enduring self-esteem and confidence based on competence when we challenge students to develop their reading and writing powers and the thinking skills which grow with them."

From "Winning Parents, Winning Children"

What Is That Thing?
Whose Stuff Is This?

By John Gile With Illustrations by Karen Gruntman

First Edition
10   9   8   7   6   5   4   3   2   1

Published by JGC/United Publishing Corps
www.jgcunited.com

Library of Congress Card Number: 00-108707
ISBN: 0-910941-27-0

Printed in the United States of America
by Worzalla, Stevens Point, Wisconsin

With gratitude to family and friends
whose kind words are a constant source
of comfort and encouragement.
J.G.

To Collin, Cameron, and New Baby
with all my love,
K.S.G.

There was a time,
  long before we were born,
    when words and names were unknown,
    when people lived in caves and trees
    and worked with tools of stone.

Back then
  we spoke in grunts and groans;
    we'd howl and growl and snort.

There were no words or names to say
and life was hard and short.

But then we learned that building fires
could make the dark night bright . . .
and warm us in the beastly cold . . .

and put wild beasts to flight.

More changes came.
We made a wheel.

We learned to build homes better.

But nothing compares
   with the changes that came
      when someone carved the first letter.

That's when words took form
and gave us power
to share what we know and discover.

With words came the power
    to read
    and write
    and talk with
    and learn from each other.

It was long, long ago
    when words were unknown
        and no one was called by name.
But what if, today,
    we lost words we say?
Nothing would be the same.

What if you had no name
and I had no name
and our friends were nameless, too?

If we wanted to meet
in a crowd on a street,
we'd just have to shout, "Hey, you!"

But "you" is nobody's name
 and everyone's name —
  so we answer, "Hey, you!" with,
   "Who, me?"
Nobody knows,
 till we say the right name,
  who it is we are seeking to see.

Even pets have names.
That's how they can know
    when we call them to come and play.

If we don't say their names,
they may not obey.
They might even run away.

Our streets have names . . .   and cities have names.

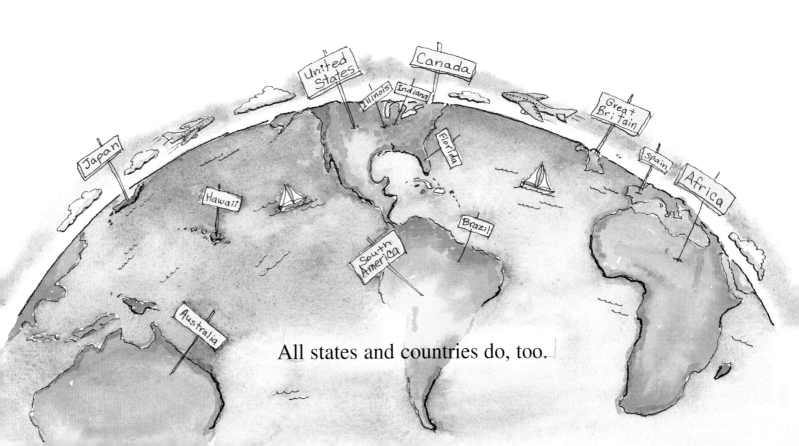

All states and countries do, too.

Their names help us know
the way to go
when we're visiting some place new.

Imagine a trip
on a train or a plane
to a place that has no name.

Is it east or west or north or south?
Without names,
    every place is the same.

And how could we pack
for our trip to that place?
Words and names
help us know
what to take.

But if all we were told
  was to pack some "things,"
    we could pack useless things by mistake.

Our clothes have names.
They're shirts and skirts
    and pants and coats and shoes.
They're mittens
    and boots
    and swimming suits.
Their names help us know
    what to choose.

And what would we eat
  on our trip to that place
    if the menu said, "Hot and cold stuff?"

We might get a plate
   filled with pebbles and bugs
     or a sandpaper sandwich that's rough.

Words and names help us choose
and get what we want —
like peanut butter and jelly,
or chocolate milk and ice cream cones —
sweet treats for any age belly.

But we need the right words
    to get what we want
        and help others understand.
If we ask for "grit"
    when we really want "grits,"
        we might get a bowl full of sand.

And what if we lost
    what we took on our trip,
        or our photos fell out of our wallets?
Who could help if we said,
    "Where's my thingamajig?"
        or, "Have you seen my whatchamacallits?"

Then, how could we know
    when we've reached that place
        with no name to tell us we're there?
Without names to guide us,
    we'd always be lost,
        anytime,
        anyplace,
        anywhere.

A name is a word
    and a word is a name
        for something we need to know.
There's a word-name for
        everything,
        everyone,
        and for everywhere we go.

There even are words
 for thoughts we think,
  and words for numbers, too.
How could we know,
 if we didn't have words,
  that one plus one makes two?

And what would become of our friends
without words?
There'd be nothing we'd share and discuss.
We need words to understand others
and help others understand us.

With words, we can share
   what's deep in our hearts
      and let others know how we feel.
Words can even help mend
   broken friendships,
      make us smile,
         and help hurt feelings heal.

Words give us power
   to learn and to grow.
They spread knowledge
   all over the place.
With words,
   we've learned how to build cars,
   to make planes,
   and put rockets in outer space!

We've come a long way
   since back in the day
      when our home was a cave or a tree.
But no limit's in sight!
Who knows what words might still
   free us to do and to be?

Quietly, steadily, word power grows,
like a tree growing out of a seed.
It's growing whenever we look in a book
and make time and take time to read.